THE THUMB RESOURCE

THE THUMB RESOURCE

David Jeb

All rights reserved. No part of this publication may be reproduced, distributed, or transmitted in any form or by any means, including photocopying, recording, or other electronic or mechanical methods, without the prior written permission of the publisher, except in the case of brief quotations embodied in critical reviews and certain other noncommercial uses permitted by copyright law.

Dedication

This book is dedicated to all my mentors, teachers, business associates, and the invaluable networks I have been privileged to be a part of, who have helped me build and sustain tangible success. Your support has been instrumental in shaping my journey and making my mark. To those who seem to have all the resources—financial, physical, technological, and human—but still find themselves stalled in their pursuits, may this book offer guidance and insights that help you unlock your full potential. I extend my heartfelt gratitude to my wife, Umu, my friends, and my family for their unwavering support throughout this journey. I could not have achieved this without you. Above all, to Him who causes us to will and to act according to His good pleasure, to Him alone be all praise and gratitude, our Father, our God, and our Maker.

"But remember the Lord your God, for it is He

who gives you the ability to produce wealth, and so confirms His covenant, which He swore to your ancestors, as it is today."

— Deuteronomy 8:18 (NIV)

Contents

	Preface	ix
1.	Networks and Relationships in Business	1
2.	Financial Resources vs. Networks: Money Can't Buy Loyalty	8
3.	Human Resources vs. Networks: The Power of Connections	18
4.	Physical Resources vs. Networks: Beyond Tangible Assets	25
5.	Knowledge Resources vs. Networks: Information Flow through Connections	32
6.	Network Foundations: Building Trust and Reciprocity	39
7.	Leveraging Customer Relationships: Turning Buyers into Advocates	44

8.	Supplier Networks: Creating Synergistic Partnerships	50
9.	Financial Networks: Relationship Capital	55
10.	Internal Networks: Enhancing Organizational Cohesion	60
11.	External Networks: Expanding Influence and Reach	65
12.	Technology and Networks: Enhancing Human Connections	70
13.	Global Networking: Crossing Borders and Cultures	75
14.	Resilience through Relationships: Navigating Crises	82
15.	The Future of Business: The Evolving Role of Networks	87
	Conclusion	95

Preface

On one of those evenings I spent with Umu (my wife), we were watching an action movie where this gang leader would punish failures by taking a finger. Out of the blue, she asked me a question that piqued my curiosity: 'Babe, which is the most important finger on your hand?' Most men would be very careful answering that question when their wives ask. I personally had no immediate answer for personal reasons. Later, when I found myself alone in the car, I asked the same question. Let's just say the responses that came to mind weren't exactly profound. But after I moved beyond the one-track mind most men might adopt, I came to a realization:

While it can vary based on context and individual needs, the thumb is generally considered the most essential. The thumb's unique opposability—its ability to touch the tips of the other fingers—enables complex hand functions such as grasping objects, writing, and using tools. This remarkable dexterity sets human hands apart from those of many other animals. During my training with the ITC

Competitiveness Section, I was introduced to the concept of five fundamental resources in business: Financial, Human, Physical, Knowledge, and Networks and Relationships.

Over the past decade, I have dedicated myself to proving the critical importance of these resources through my investment and entrepreneurial experiences. The importance of various resources can depend on the business type, industry, and specific circumstances. Many argue that Human resources are paramount. Skilled and motivated employees drive innovation, productivity, and customer satisfaction. They manage and optimize other resources, making human capital a key asset for any organization. While financial, physical, knowledge, and network resources are all vital, it is ultimately people who leverage these resources to create value, solve problems, and drive growth.

However, in today's interconnected world, our networks and relationships—customers, suppliers, financiers—are indispensable. Our physical resources—computers, cars, machinery—exist to support these networks. While information and knowhow were once crucial, the advent of AI has shifted their importance. Thus, in this context, networks and relationships emerge as the most crucial resources of all. I am excited to elevate your views about the resources of business in this book, "The Thumb Resource." Like the thumb on a hand, networks and relationships are central, enabling and enhancing the function of all other resources. Every other resource revolves around their significance.

Join me as we explore why networks and relationships are the cornerstone of business success, and discover how to leverage them effectively to propel your ventures forward.

I.

Networks and Relationships in Business

In the dynamic landscape of modern business, success is increasingly dependent not just on individual competence or the strength of a company's internal operations, but also on the breadth and quality of its networks and relationships. These networks encompass connections with customers, suppliers, industry peers, and various other stakeholders. Relationships in business are foundational to collaboration, innovation, and growth, playing a critical role in navigating the complexities of the market.

In "*Love Leadership: The New Way to Lead in a Fear- Based World*," John Hope Bryant emphasizes the paramount importance of networks and relationships, stating, "Building relationships is the most important thing we can do, as individuals and organizations, because relationships are the only thing that truly lasts." While businesses may face bankruptcy, employees may resign, assets can be seized, and information may evolve, a steadfast relationship offers a foundation to rebuild. A well-established and loyal network possesses the transformative power to overcome even the most difficult challenges .

The Concept of Networks in Business

Networks in business refer to the web of connections and interactions between individuals and organizations. These connections can be formal or informal and span different levels of professional interactions, from partnerships and alliances to mentorships and customer relationships. Reginald F. Lewis and his company, TLC Beatrice International Holdings, Inc., exemplify the power of business networks in Black American history. In 1987, Lewis led the leveraged buyout of Beatrice International Foods for $985 million, marking the largest such deal outside the U.S. at the time. This success was made possible through formal networks of investors, legal advisors, and financial institutions, all governed by clear contracts and agreements.

Lewis also benefited from informal networks, drawing on mentorship and personal relationships with influential business figures. These connections provided him with valuable advice and support, contributing to his strategic decision-making. Internally, he promoted a culture of collaboration within TLC Beatrice, encouraging employees to share knowledge and best practices across departments, which enhanced both efficiency and innovation. Externally, Lewis built strong relationships with suppliers, customers, and industry influencers, expanding TLC Beatrice's market reach and intelligence. Externally, Lewis nurtured strong relationships with suppliers, customers, and industry influencers. These networks were essential in expanding TLC Beatrice's market reach and intelligence. His external connections were pivotal in navigating international markets and identifying growth opportunities.

Formal Networks include structured partnerships and alliances, where businesses work together towards common goals. Examples include strategic partnerships, joint ventures, and industry consortia. Formal networks are often governed by contracts and formal agreements, ensuring clear expectations and commitments.

Informal Networks are less structured and include relationships built on personal interactions and mutual interests. Informal networks can be just as valuable as formal ones, facilitating knowledge sharing, advice, and support that are not bound by contractual obligations.

Within an organization, networks among employees across different departments can enhance collaboration, foster innovation, and improve efficiency. Internal networks ensure that knowledge and best practices are shared across the organization, leading to better decision-making and problem- solving. External Networks on the other hand include connections with entities outside the organization, such as customers, suppliers, competitors, and industry influencers. They expand a company's reach and provide opportunities for growth, market intelligence, and strategic partnerships.

The Relevance

Networks enable businesses to access a broader pool of knowledge and expertise. Collaboration with diverse stakeholders brings in new ideas and perspectives, fostering innovation. For instance, partnerships with research institutions can lead to ground-breaking technological advancements. Strong networks open doors to new markets and customer segments. Businesses can leverage their relationships to enter new geographical areas or industries, gaining a competitive edge. For example, partnerships with local distributors can facilitate entry into foreign markets.

Trust is a critical component of successful business relationships. Networks built on trust and mutual respect enhance a company's credibility and reputation. This trust can lead to long-term customer loyalty, favorable terms with suppliers, and supportive alliances. John Bryant Hope, has written extensively about the importance of trust in business relationships. In his book, "Love Leadership: The New Way to Lead in a Fear-Based World", he emphasizes how trust and mutual respect are essential for building successful networks. "Trust is the foundation upon which all meaningful relationships are built. Without trust, there can be no genuine connection, no true collaboration, and no lasting success."

Breaking it down later he says, "In business,

trust is not just a nice-to-have; it's a must-have. It is the bedrock that supports every interaction, every partnership, and every deal. When we lead with love and integrity, we cultivate trust naturally. Customers come back because they believe in our promises. Suppliers offer favourable terms because they know we will honour our commitments. Allies stand by us because they respect our values. Trust transforms business relationships from mere transactions into enduring partnerships. It is this trust that ultimately fuels sustainable success and growth in the marketplace."

Trust is indispensable for creating and establishing networks that enhance a business's credibility, reputation, and longevity.

Through these networks, businesses can share resources, reduce costs and optimize operations. Collaborative ventures enable companies to pool their strengths and mitigate risks. For example, companies within a supply chain network can collectively negotiate better terms or share logistics infrastructure.

Businesses face a myriad of challenges, including regulatory changes, technological disruptions, and economic fluctuations. Strong networks provide the support and flexibility needed to navigate these complexities. Peer networks, industry groups, and professional associations offer valuable platforms for shared learning and collective problem-solving. Networks play a crucial role in attracting and retaining top talent. Professional relationships and industry connections help businesses identify and recruit skilled individuals. Moreover, a networked organization that fosters strong internal relationships tends to have higher employee satisfaction and retention rates. Networks and relationships are indispensable assets in the modern business world. They provide the foundation for innovation, growth, and sustainability. By cultivating strong, trust-based relationships both within and outside the organization, businesses can unlock new opportunities, enhance their market position, and build resilience against the challenges of an ever-evolving marketplace. Emphasizing the strategic development and management of networks will continue to be a key driver of success in the increasingly interconnected business environment.

2.

Financial Resources vs. Networks: Money Can't Buy Loyalty

The Value of Relationships with Customers, Suppliers, and Investors Over Financial Capital

In the realm of business, financial capital is traditionally viewed as the cornerstone of growth and sustainability. However, in an era defined by rapid change and interconnectedness, the importance of relationships–specifically with customers, suppliers, and investors–often surpasses the value of financial resources. These relationships provide intangible assets that foster long-term success, resilience, and competitive advantage. The place of financial capital as paramount for growth and sustainability cannot be denied. However, Tyler Perry's journey to build a new Hollywood in Atlanta, Georgia, reveals a deeper truth: relationships often outweigh mere financial resources. His ascent exemplifies this, as he strategically leveraged alliances, partnerships, and visionary financiers who believed in his talent and potential. Tyler's journey began by fostering deep connections with his audience through stage plays that resonated with African American communities. This loyal fan base provided the foundation for his transition into television and film, facilitating long-term customer loyalty and significant box office success. He forged strategic partnerships with industry suppliers, including actors, crew members, and production companies, cementing alliances that were crucial for his studio's growth.

One pivotal ally in Perry's journey was media mogul Oprah Winfrey, who offered him a platform on her OWN Network in 2006 to produce scripted television shows, expanding his reach to a broader audience. Additionally, Perry formed a fruitful partnership with Lionsgate, a major entertainment company, collaborating on numerous film projects, including the iconic "Madea" series. Lionsgate provided both distribution and financial backing, enabling Perry's ventures to flourish. Financial support was substantially garnered from private investors and institutions like JP Morgan Chase, all of which had established standing relations with Tyler. This backing was instrumental in acquiring and developing the historic Fort McPherson military base into Tyler Perry Studios' sprawling campus, further solidifying Atlanta's status as a burgeoning film production hub. Through adept navigation of these relationships, Perry transformed Atlanta's landscape, showcasing the enduring power of connections in surpassing mere financial resources on the path to long-term success and sustainability in the entertainment industry.

Relationships with Customers

Building strong relationships with customers leads to loyalty and repeat business, which are more cost- effective than acquiring new customers. A loyal customer base provides a steady revenue stream and valuable word-of-mouth promotion. "Lasting relationships can never be bought, they can only be built.", Dr. Robert Holden, a British psychologist, author, and expert in the field of positive psychology and well-being. He emphasizes the importance of authentic connections and the idea that genuine relationships cannot be purchased but must be nurtured and cultivated over time through trust, mutual respect, and shared experiences. Engaged customers will always offer critical insights into their needs, preferences, and pain points. This feedback is essential for refining products, services, and customer experiences. By staying attuned to customer feedback, businesses can innovate more effectively and remain relevant in the market. Satisfied and delighted customers often become brand advocates, promoting the company to others. This organic marketing can be more influential and trustworthy than traditional advertising, significantly enhancing a brand's reputation and reach.

Relationships with Suppliers
Strong supplier relationships ensure a reliable supply of high-quality materials and services. When suppliers are treated as partners rather than mere vendors, they are more likely to prioritize the company's needs, ensuring better quality control and consistency.

Collaborative relationships with suppliers can lead to innovations in the supply chain, such as cost-saving measures, new product development, and improved logistics. Suppliers who feel valued and engaged are more likely to invest in these innovations, benefiting both parties. In 2009, Nestlé embarked on a significant journey in Côte d'Ivoire with the launch of the Nestlé Cocoa Plan. This initiative aimed to improve the livelihoods of cocoa farmers and ensure a sustainable cocoa supply chain. Nestlé began working directly with thousands of cocoa farmers, providing them with training on sustainable farming practices and access to high- yield and disease-resistant cocoa plant varieties. This collaboration fostered innovations that significantly improved farm productivity and cocoa quality.

Over the next decade, the impact of the Nestlé Cocoa Plan became evident. By 2019, the initiative had distributed millions of higher-yielding cocoa plants, leading to a substantial increase in yields for participating farmers, significantly boosting their incomes. For Nestlé, this meant a more stable and high-quality cocoa supply, essential for their wide range of chocolate products. The improved quality and sustainability of the cocoa allowed Nestlé to market their products with a strong emphasis on ethical and sustainable sourcing, catering to the growing consumer demand for responsibly sourced goods.

Nestlé's investment didn't stop at the farms. The company also focused on developing better infrastructure and supply chain logistics. By 2020, Nestlé had built or renovated numerous schools and provided water wells in cocoa-growing communities, benefiting tens of thousands of people. These investments reduced the time and cost of transporting cocoa from farms to processing facilities, improving overall supply chain efficiency. This collaborative relationship with the farmers encouraged them to adopt better practices, leading to mutual benefits and fostering innovation within the supply chain.

In times of disruption, such as economic downturns or supply chain crises, solid relationships with suppliers can provide a buffer. Suppliers are more likely to offer flexible terms, prioritize delivery, and collaborate on problem-solving when they have a strong, trust-based relationship with the company.

Relationships with Investors

Investors who have a strong relationship with a company are more likely to provide continued support through various stages of growth. They are often willing to offer financial backing during challenging times, ensuring stability and confidence in the business.

Beyond capital, investors often bring valuable expertise, industry knowledge, and strategic guidance. Their experience can help steer the company through complex decisions, market expansions, and strategic pivots. In 2013, the Italian agribusiness company Eataly secured investment from Tamburi Investment Partners (TIP), an Italian investment firm known for its strategic guidance and industry expertise. TIP didn't just bring capital to Eataly; they brought a wealth of experience and knowledge in retail expansion and global market penetration. With TIP's backing, Eataly was able to navigate complex decisions and strategically expand its operations, opening new locations in major cities worldwide, including New York, Tokyo, and São Paulo. This partnership proved invaluable when Eataly faced the challenge of maintaining its authentic Italian market experience while scaling up internationally. TIP's strategic guidance helped Eataly adapt to diverse markets without compromising its brand integrity. Their expertise in retail and consumer behavior enabled Eataly to make informed decisions about store locations, product offerings, and marketing strategies. As a result, Eataly successfully established itself as a global brand, demonstrating how investor expertise can significantly impact a company's growth and strategic direction. Investors typically have extensive networks that can open doors to new opportunities, partnerships, and markets. By leveraging these connections, businesses can accelerate growth and gain a competitive edge that financial capital alone cannot provide.

The Comparative Value of Relationships Over Financial Capital

While financial capital is essential for operations and growth, relationships create a sustainable competitive advantage that is harder to replicate. Competitors can match or exceed financial investments, but replicating the depth and quality of established relationships is far more challenging. Strong relationships with customers, suppliers, and investors contribute to organizational resilience. They provide a support system that helps navigate uncertainties, adapt to changes, and recover from setbacks more effectively than financial resources alone.

Trust, built through relationships, is a critical asset in business. A company known for its strong relationships is perceived as more trustworthy and reputable. This reputation attracts new customers, partners, and investors, creating a virtuous cycle of growth and stability. In the German pharmaceutical industry, Bayer AG's longstanding commitment to building strong relationships with healthcare professionals, patients, and regulatory bodies has established it as a trusted and reputable entity. This trust was particularly evident in 2016 when Bayer acquired Monsanto. Despite the controversy surrounding Monsanto, Bayer's solid reputation helped mitigate concerns and secure stakeholder support. Bayer's consistent engagement and transparency fostered trust, attracting new partnerships and investments. This virtuous cycle of trust and credibility has enabled Bayer to expand its global footprint, innovate in healthcare solutions, and maintain stability amidst industry challenges.

Financial capital is undeniably crucial for business operations and expansion, but the value of relationships with customers, suppliers, and investors often outweighs mere monetary resources. These relationships foster loyalty, innovation, flexibility, and resilience, providing a competitive edge that financial capital alone cannot achieve. By prioritizing and nurturing these relationships, businesses can build a strong, sustainable foundation that supports long- term success and growth in an increasingly interconnected and dynamic market.

3.

Human Resources vs. Networks: The Power of Connections

During the Black Slave days in the 19th century, the Underground Railroad exemplified the power of professional networks in shaping an organization's human capital. This covert network of abolitionists, free Black individuals, and sympathetic allies worked together to discover, engage, and nurture the talents of those escaping slavery. Through secret routes and safe houses, they connected runaways with opportunities for freedom and self-sufficiency in the North. These networks not only provided immediate support and safety but also helped the formerly enslaved integrate into new communities, leveraging their skills and potential to build lives of dignity and contribute to the economic and social fabric of their new homes. Powerful connections and networks can be invaluable in uncovering and fostering human potential, even in the most challenging circumstances. Beyond traditional recruitment methods, professional networks play a pivotal role in shaping an organization's human capital. These networks, comprising both internal and external connections, serve as vital channels for discovering, engaging, and nurturing talented individuals.

Attracting Top Talent
Professional networks significantly expand the reach of job postings and company branding. Platforms like LinkedIn and industry-specific forums allow businesses to tap into a global talent pool. By leveraging the networks of current employees, companies can broadcast job openings to a wider, more relevant audience, increasing the chances of attracting high-quality candidates. A strong employer brand is a magnet for top talent. Networks play a crucial role in shaping and communicating this brand. Employee testimonials, social media presence, and industry partnerships all contribute to an attractive image. When professionals see an organization actively engaged in its community and industry, they are more likely to consider

it a desirable place to work. Of course, there are always those who prioritize the size of the paycheck over other factors. Employee referrals are one of the most effective recruitment tools, often leading to faster hires and better cultural fit. Networks facilitate these referrals by connecting potential candidates with current employees. When trusted colleagues or industry peers recommend an organization, it significantly boosts its attractiveness to top talent.

Retaining Top Talent

In the early 2000s, Skadden, Arps, Slate, Meagher & Flom LLP, a New York City based firm, with offices located in major cities including London, Los Angeles, Washington D.C. and many others, initiated efforts to cultivate a supportive and inclusive culture within the firm. They introduced mentorship programs, affinity groups, and regular team-building activities to address the demanding nature of legal work and foster a sense of belonging among employees. As a result of these initiatives, Skadden experienced significantly lower turnover rates, with many associates and partners opting to build long-term careers at the firm. This investment in employee well-being and professional development not only enhanced retention but also contributed to a more cohesive and engaged workforce, ultimately strengthening the firm's competitive edge in the legal sector.

Retention is closely linked to an employee's sense of belonging and connection within the organization. Internal networks foster this sense of community, helping employees build relationships beyond their immediate teams. Social events, cross-departmental projects, and mentorship programs strengthen these internal networks, enhancing job satisfaction and loyalty.

Networks provide a support system that helps employees navigate challenges and find solutions more efficiently. Access to a network of knowledgeable colleagues and external industry experts enables employees to grow and succeed in their roles. This support network can be particularly valuable during times of change or stress, reinforcing an employee's decision to stay with the company. Professional growth is a key factor in retention. Networks provide avenues for career development through mentorship, learning opportunities, and exposure to new ideas. Internal networks connect employees with mentors and career coaches who can guide their development. External networks offer access to industry trends, conferences, and professional groups that broaden employees' perspectives and skills.

Developing Top Talent

Well-knit networks facilitate the flow of knowledge both within and outside the organization. By fostering a culture of collaboration, organizations ensure that valuable insights and expertise are shared across departments and teams. This collaborative environment is essential for the continuous development of top talent, encouraging them to innovate and excel. In the early 2000s, at the height of the dot-com bubble, Google faced a critical infrastructure challenge that threatened the company's operations. In a remarkable turn of events, an employee named Urs Hölzle, who had initially been hired as a software engineer, emerged as the unlikely hero. Hölzle, known for his deep understanding of computer systems and networking, had been quietly networking within the company and had built a reputation for his expertise. When Google encountered a sudden surge in user traffic that its servers couldn't handle, Hölzle's informal network and technical prowess proved invaluable. Drawing on his connections and knowledge, he quickly devised innovative solutions to scale Google's infrastructure, ensuring the company's survival during this critical period. Identifying high-potential employees who might otherwise go unnoticed will sometimes require trusted but uncelebrated networks.

These informal networks often reveal talents and skills that formal assessments might miss. Once identified, these individuals can be nurtured through targeted development programs, leadership training, and stretch assignments that prepare them for higher responsibilities. Effective mentorship is a cornerstone of talent development. Networks connect employees with mentors who can provide guidance, feedback, and inspiration. These relationships are invaluable for personal and professional growth, helping employees navigate their careers and achieve their goals. Access to role models within the network also motivates employees by showing them the potential career paths and achievements they can aspire to. Networks play an indispensable role in attracting, retaining, and developing top talent. They broaden the reach and appeal of recruitment efforts, foster a supportive and engaging work environment, and provide crucial opportunities for growth and development. By actively cultivating and leveraging these networks, organizations can build a robust talent pipeline, ensure employee satisfaction and loyalty, and drive continuous improvement and innovation. In an increasingly interconnected world, the strategic use of professional networks is not just an advantage but a necessity for sustained organizational success.

4.

Physical Resources vs. Networks: Beyond Tangible Assets

Had it not been for General Motors' strategic partnerships during their struggles in the recent EV market stampede, the company might not have weathered the storm as effectively. A key partnership in this context was with LG Chem, a leading battery manufacturer. Their collaboration led to the development of the Chevrolet Bolt, a pivotal electric vehicle offering affordability and long-range capabilities. GM tapped into LG Chem's expertise in battery technology, ensuring the Bolt's competitive edge. GM's alliances with government agencies and local communities also facilitated the establishment of charging infrastructure and supportive policies, further boosting the adoption of electric vehicles. These partnerships underscore the critical role of relationships in driving innovation and sustainability, ultimately enabling General Motors to emerge as a key player in sustainable transportation despite the market challenges.

Relationships play a crucial role in enhancing the utility and effectiveness of physical resources by fostering collaboration, improving resource management, and promoting sustainable practices. The interconnectedness of individuals, organizations, and communities enables more efficient and innovative use of resources, maximizing their potential and ensuring their benefits are widely distributed.

Firstly, collaboration arising from strong relationships can lead to more effective use of physical resources. When individuals or organizations work together, they can share knowledge, skills, and technologies that optimize resource utilization. For example, in agricultural communities, farmers often share insights and techniques that improve crop yields and reduce waste. Similarly, businesses can collaborate through partnerships or supply chains to streamline operations and reduce costs. By pooling resources and expertise, relationships help achieve outcomes that would be difficult or impossible in isolation. Moreover, effective management of physical resources often depends on the strength of relationships within and between organizations. Good communication and trust among team members or departments facilitate better planning and coordination. For instance, in construction projects, the synergy between architects, engineers, and contractors ensures that materials are used efficiently, timelines are met, and budgets are adhered to. This cooperation minimizes delays and maximizes the quality and longevity of the built environment. Relationships also promote innovation, which enhances the utility of physical resources. Collaborative efforts in research and development can lead to new technologies and methods that make better use of existing resources. For example, in the energy sector, partnerships between research institutions and industry have led to advancements in renewable energy technologies, such as solar panels and wind turbines. These innovations not only improve the efficiency of energy production but also reduce the environmental impact, making the use of physical resources more sustainable.

Sustainability is another significant area where relationships enhance the utility and effectiveness of physical resources. The global nature of environmental challenges necessitates cooperation across borders and sectors. International agreements and partnerships, such as the Paris Agreement on climate change, are essential for coordinating efforts to manage natural resources responsibly.

These relationships enable countries to share best practices, provide financial and technical support to one another, and commit to joint actions that preserve resources for future generations. On a community level, relationships are fundamental in promoting sustainable practices. Local networks and organizations often spearhead initiatives that encourage recycling, conservation, and the responsible use of resources. Community gardens, for instance, bring people together to grow food locally, reducing the need for transportation and promoting self-sufficiency. These initiatives rely on the strength of relationships among community members to succeed and have a lasting impact. Furthermore, relationships can help mitigate conflicts over resource use. In areas where resources are scarce, strong relationships and effective communication channels can lead to cooperative solutions that benefit all parties involved. For example, water-sharing agreements between neighbouring regions or countries can prevent disputes and ensure that water is allocated fairly and used efficiently. Such agreements are often the result of long-term diplomatic efforts and mutual understanding, underscoring the importance of relationships in resource management. Tensions over the Nile River have prominently involved Egypt, Sudan, and Ethiopia, particularly due to Ethiopia's construction of the Grand Ethiopian Renaissance Dam (GERD) initiated in 2011. This project aimed to enhance Ethiopia's electricity generation, but Egypt and Sudan raised concerns about potential impacts on their water supplies. To address these concerns, international organizations and regional alliances, such as the African Union (AU) and the Nile Basin Initiative (NBI), facilitated numerous negotiations. A significant milestone was the Declaration of Principles signed in March 2015 by Egypt, Sudan, and Ethiopia, which established cooperation guidelines for the dam's filling and operation.

Despite the 2015 agreement, disputes continued, leading to further talks mediated by the AU, the United States, and the World Bank in 2020 and 2021. These negotiations emphasized equitable and reasonable utilization of the Nile's waters, balancing Ethiopia's developmental needs with Egypt's and Sudan's water security concerns. While a comprehensive resolution has yet to be fully achieved, the ongoing dialogue facilitated by international networks and diplomatic channels underscores the importance of cooperation in managing shared resources. The efforts highlight how strong relationships and effective communication can help transform potential conflicts into cooperative solutions, benefiting all parties involved.

Trusted tested relationships significantly enhance the utility and effectiveness of physical resources by fostering collaboration, improving management, promoting innovation, supporting sustainability, and mitigating conflicts. The interconnected nature of modern society means that no individual or organization can operate in isolation. By building and maintaining strong relationships, we can ensure that physical resources are used in ways that maximize their potential and benefit society as a whole. These relationships are the bedrock of progress, enabling us to tackle complex challenges and create a more sustainable and equitable future.

5.

Knowledge Resources vs. Networks: Information Flow through Connections

During the gold rush in Europe in the mid-19th century, the Rothschild banking family exemplified the power of networks in gaining critical business knowledge and insights. With branches across major European financial centres, the Rothschilds established an extensive network that spanned continents. This network enabled them to gather timely information about gold discoveries, market trends, and geopolitical developments, giving them a significant advantage in the financial markets. For instance, during the California Gold Rush of 1848-1855, the Rothschilds' network allowed them to swiftly capitalize on the surge in demand for gold, facilitating lucrative investments in mining ventures and commodities trading. By leveraging their extensive network, the Rothschilds not only accumulated wealth but also wielded considerable influence in shaping financial markets and economic policies. Their ability to tap into diverse networks enabled them to stay ahead of competitors and adapt to changing market conditions, highlighting the enduring importance of networks in gaining critical business insights and maintaining a competitive edge in dynamic environments. Networks play a pivotal role in the sharing and acquisition of critical business knowledge and insights, serving as conduits for information exchange, collaboration, and professional development.

In today's fast-paced and interconnected business landscape, the ability to tap into diverse networks can provide a competitive edge and facilitate both individual and organizational success. Firstly, networks offer a platform for the dissemination of knowledge and insights among professionals within an industry or field. Through various channels such as industry conferences, trade associations, and online forums, individuals can share best practices, emerging trends, and lessons learned from their experiences. This exchange of information helps to build a collective knowledge base and enables practitioners to stay abreast of developments in their respective domains. Also, networks facilitate collaboration and knowledge co-creation among diverse stakeholders. By connecting individuals with complementary expertise or resources, networks enable synergies that lead to innovative solutions to complex problems. Collaborative projects, joint ventures, and partnerships formed within networks leverage the strengths of multiple parties, resulting in more robust outcomes than would be achievable independently. For example, in the technology sector, cross-industry collaborations between software developers, hardware manufacturers, and end-users drive the advancement of cutting-edge products and services.

In addition to sharing knowledge horizontally within industries, networks also enable vertical knowledge transfer across different sectors and disciplines. Interdisciplinary networks bring together professionals from diverse backgrounds, such as engineering, finance, marketing, and law, to exchange perspectives and insights on common challenges. This cross-pollination of ideas fosters creativity and innovation by introducing fresh perspectives and alternative approaches to problem-solving. For instance, in the healthcare industry, collaborations between medical researchers, technology experts, and policymakers have led to breakthroughs in treatments, diagnostics, and healthcare delivery models.

Furthermore, networks serve as valuable sources of mentorship and professional development for individuals at all stages of their careers. Mentors within networks provide guidance, advice, and support based on their own experiences, helping mentees navigate career transitions, overcome obstacles, and develop essential skills. Similarly, peer-to-peer learning within networks enables individuals to learn from their colleagues' successes and failures, gaining practical insights that complement formal education and training programs. As a result, professionals can continuously enhance their competencies and adapt to evolving industry dynamics. Beyond individual benefits, networks also offer strategic advantages for organizations seeking to stay ahead in today's competitive marketplace. By fostering strong relationships with customers, suppliers, and industry influencers, businesses can gain valuable market intelligence, identify emerging opportunities, and anticipate industry trends. Moreover, networks provide access to talent pools, investment opportunities, and strategic partnerships that can fuel growth and expansion initiatives. In essence, organizations that cultivate extensive and diverse networks are better positioned to innovate, adapt, and thrive in dynamic business environments.

Business Intelligence, insights, and critical knowledge are essential facets of modern business and organizational success. Networks serve as vital conduits for their sharing and acquisition, empowering professionals and organizations to remain competitive and realize their objectives. In the heart of Chicago, amidst the challenges of urban violence, one organization stands out for its unwavering commitment to combatting this issue at the grassroots level: Fierce Women of Faith (FWF). Led by their visionary founder and Chairperson, Dr. Mercenia J. Richards. FWF has emerged as a beacon of hope, employing innovative strategies and collaborative partnerships to address the root causes of violence in the community.

At the core of FWF's approach is the recognition that true change comes from within the community itself. In the spirit of networks and relationships, FWF has actively engaged with gang and ring leaders, forging unlikely alliances to reduce violence on the streets. This bold initiative has not only fostered trust and dialogue but has also empowered these leaders to become agents of positive change within their own communities. Through their collaborative efforts, FWF has implemented a range of impactful programs and initiatives aimed at addressing the underlying factors contributing to violence. From mentoring and job training to community outreach and conflict resolution, FWF is dedicated to providing individuals with the tools and support they need to break the cycle of violence and build brighter futures.

The results of FWF's efforts are tangible and far- reaching. Since their inception, they have witnessed a significant reduction in violence in Chicago and Cook County. By fostering a culture of empowerment, collaboration, and resilience, FWF has not only transformed the lives of countless individuals but has also helped to create safer and more vibrant communities for all. In the face of adversity, Fierce Women of Faith (FWF) continues to stand as a testament to the power of community-led initiatives and the transformative potential of networks and relationships. Through their innovative approach and unwavering commitment, FWF is reshaping the narrative of violence in Chicago and inspiring hope for a brighter future.

In the past year alone, over 100 victims and perpetrators of violence in Chicago have found solace and a platform for their stories through Fierce Women of Faith (FWF)'s 'Safe Spaces' project, generously funded by the Carl R. Hendrickson Family Foundation. Through podcasts and interviews, their narratives shed light on the harsh realities of violence, with FWF's efforts culminating in a compilation of lessons learned set for television broadcast, aiming to ignite awareness and action for a safer Chicago. By facilitating information exchange, collaboration, mentorship, and strategic partnerships, networks empower individuals to leverage collective intelligence, drive innovation, and navigate complex challenges. In an era defined by rapid change and uncertainty, the ability to tap into diverse networks is a valuable asset that can spell the difference between success and stagnation in the business world.

6.

Network Foundations: Building Trust and Reciprocity

The story of Ecobank began with the vision of George A. Elombi, a Cameroonian banker, who sought to create a pan-African financial institution that would cater to the diverse needs of the continent. In 1985, he founded Ecobank in Togo, with the aim of leveraging networks within Africa to provide accessible banking services and drive economic development. Elombi's visionary leadership and commitment to serving Africa's communities laid the foundation for Ecobank's growth and success. Throughout the 1990s and early 2000s, Ecobank expanded its footprint across Africa, establishing branches and subsidiaries in multiple countries. By harnessing networks within Africa, Ecobank fostered strong relationships with local communities, businesses, and governments, earning a reputation as a trusted financial partner. Under the leadership of Arnold Ekpe, who served as CEO from 2005 to 2012, Ecobank further solidified its position as one of the most trusted banks on the continent. Ekpe's strategic vision and emphasis on innovation propelled Ecobank's growth, enabling it to serve millions of customers across Africa.

In 2008, Ecobank made history by becoming the first sub-Saharan African bank to list on the London Stock Exchange, showcasing its resilience and credibility on the global stage. Through its extensive network of branches, partnerships, and alliances, Ecobank continues to play a pivotal role in driving financial inclusion and economic growth across Africa.

Building strong business relationships relies on fundamental principles of trust and reciprocity, which form the bedrock of successful collaborations, partnerships, and transactions. In today's interconnected and fast-paced business environment, establishing and maintaining trust is essential for fostering long-term relationships that drive mutual benefit and growth. Trust is the cornerstone of any meaningful relationship, whether personal or professional. In the business context, trust is built upon a foundation of integrity, reliability, and transparency. When individuals and organizations demonstrate honesty and ethical behavior in their interactions, they earn the confidence and respect of their counterparts. This trust forms the basis for open communication, cooperation, and collaboration, as parties feel secure in their interactions and confident in each other's intentions. Transparency plays a crucial role in fostering trust in business relationships. Open and honest communication about goals, expectations, and challenges builds credibility and reduces misunderstandings or conflicts. By sharing relevant information openly and proactively, parties demonstrate their commitment to fairness and integrity, laying the groundwork for productive and mutually beneficial partnerships.

Reliability is another key component of trust in business relationships. Consistently delivering on promises, meeting deadlines, and honouring commitments build confidence and reliability. When parties can depend on each other to fulfil their obligations, they can work together with peace of mind, knowing that they are working towards shared goals in a dependable partnership. Reciprocity is the principle of mutual exchange and cooperation that underpins strong business relationships. At its core, reciprocity involves giving and receiving support, assistance, and resources in a balanced and equitable manner. When both parties contribute value and demonstrate a willingness to help each other succeed, trust and goodwill are reinforced, strengthening the relationship over time. Reciprocity fosters a sense of fairness in business relationships, ensuring that both parties benefit from their interactions. Whether it's sharing expertise, providing referrals, or offering assistance in times of need, acts of reciprocity create a virtuous cycle of mutual support and collaboration. By recognizing and rewarding the contributions of others, businesses can cultivate a culture of reciprocity that fosters trust and cooperation among stakeholders. Moreover, reciprocity extends beyond individual transactions to encompass long-term relationships and partnerships. Investing in the success of others, even if there is no immediate benefit, can yield dividends in the form of goodwill, loyalty, and trust. By prioritizing the long-term health of relationships over short-term gains, businesses can foster a sense of mutual respect and commitment that transcends individual transactions.

During the Ebola outbreak in West Africa in 2014, Ecobank took swift and decisive action to support affected communities across the region. The bank provided financial assistance and resources to local governments and health organizations to combat the spread of the virus. Additionally, Ecobank implemented measures to ensure the safety and well- being of its employees and customers, including the distribution of hygiene kits and educational materials. When businesses contribute to the well-being of society, they build stronger relationships with their customers and communities. This is reciprocity! Trust and reciprocity are fundamental principles that underpin strong business relationships. By prioritizing integrity, transparency, reliability, and reciprocity in their interactions, individuals and organizations can build trust, foster cooperation, and drive mutual success. In an increasingly interconnected and competitive business landscape, investing in relationships based on trust and reciprocity is essential for building resilient, sustainable, and prosperous enterprises.

7.

Leveraging Customer Relationships: Turning Buyers into Advocates

In Uganda's telecom arena, the emergence of MTN Uganda as a formidable competitor challenged the incumbent, Uganda Telecom (UTL). Despite UTL's historical presence, it struggled to adapt to the changing landscape and meet the evolving needs of its customer base. As MTN Uganda gained traction with its innovative services and aggressive marketing, UTL faced declining market share and waning customer loyalty. In response, UTL attempted to deepen its customer relationships by rolling out loyalty programs and enhancing its service offerings. However, internal challenges, including operational inefficiencies and management issues, hindered its efforts to effectively engage and retain customers. Despite these endeavours, UTL found itself unable to compete effectively against the dynamic strategies of MTN Uganda.

MTN Uganda revolutionized the telecom market with its innovative strategies that propelled it to the forefront of competition. Leveraging its extensive network infrastructure and forward-thinking approach, MTN Uganda introduced a range of compelling services tailored to meet the diverse needs of customers. One of its killer strategies was its relentless focus on affordability, offering competitive pricing plans and value-added services that appealed to a wide demographic. Additionally, MTN Uganda capitalized on the rising demand for mobile data by investing heavily in its data network infrastructure, ensuring fast and reliable internet access for its subscribers. Furthermore, the company differentiated itself through aggressive marketing campaigns, strategic partnerships, and continuous technological advancements, cementing its position as a leader in the Ugandan telecommunications industry. These killer strategies not only fuelled MTN Uganda's rapid growth but also solidified its reputation as a trailblazer in innovation and customer-centricity in the region.

Ultimately, UTL's failure to adapt to the evolving market dynamics and strengthen its customer relationships led to its decline in the face of fierce competition. Deepening customer relationships is essential for sustained business growth, as loyal and engaged customers are more likely to repeat purchases, advocate for the brand, and contribute to long-term profitability. By implementing effective strategies to nurture and strengthen these relationships, businesses can enhance customer satisfaction, loyalty, and lifetime value. One strategy to deepen customer relationships is to prioritize personalized experiences and interactions. By leveraging customer data and insights, businesses can tailor their products, services, and communications to meet the individual needs and preferences of each customer. Personalization can take many forms, including personalized recommendations, targeted promotions, and customized communication channels. By demonstrating an understanding of their customers' preferences and interests, businesses can foster a sense of connection and relevance that enhances the overall customer experience.

Another strategy is to prioritize customer

engagement and communication across multiple touch points. Building strong relationships requires ongoing interaction and dialogue between the business and its customers. This can include proactive outreach through email, social media, and other digital channels, as well as responsive customer support and feedback mechanisms. By staying connected and accessible to their customers, businesses can demonstrate their commitment to customer satisfaction and responsiveness, building trust and loyalty in the process. Additionally, businesses can deepen customer relationships by delivering exceptional value and service at every opportunity. This means consistently exceeding customer expectations in terms of product quality, performance, and support. By focusing on delivering value and solving customer problems, businesses can differentiate themselves from competitors and build a reputation for excellence that attracts and retains loyal customers. Moreover, by actively seeking and acting on customer feedback, businesses can continuously improve their products and services to better meet customer needs and preferences over time.

Building a sense of community and belonging

can also be a powerful strategy for deepening customer relationships. By creating opportunities for customers to connect with each other, share experiences, and engage with the brand on a deeper level, businesses can foster a sense of belonging and loyalty that goes beyond transactional relationships. This can include hosting events, facilitating online forums and communities, and encouraging user-generated content and reviews. By nurturing a community of passionate advocates and brand ambassadors, businesses can leverage the power of word-of-mouth marketing and social proof to attract new customers and drive sustained growth.

Finally, businesses can deepen customer relationships by demonstrating a genuine commitment to social responsibility and ethical business practices. Today's consumers increasingly expect businesses to not only deliver value and convenience but also to act in ways that align with their values and beliefs. By supporting causes and initiatives that matter to their customers, businesses can demonstrate their commitment to making a positive impact on society and the environment, building trust and loyalty in the process. Deepening customer relationships is essential for sustained business growth. By prioritizing personalized experiences, proactive communication, exceptional value, community-building, and social responsibility, businesses can foster strong connections with their customers that drive loyalty, advocacy, and long-term profitability. In an increasingly competitive and customer-centric marketplace, investing in strategies to deepen customer relationships is essential for building a resilient and successful business that stands the test of time.

8.

Supplier Networks: Creating Synergistic Partnerships

In a strategic move aimed at maximizing the value of their natural resources, several African governments, predominantly those with significant mining sectors, embarked on a bold initiative: banning the export of raw earth elements and minerals. Among these precious commodities were gold, lithium, and various other elements crucial for modern industries. These governments recognized the potential for greater economic benefits by processing these minerals domestically rather than simply exporting them in their raw form. The decision was not without controversy, as it sparked debates about job creation, technological capacity, and potential trade disruptions.

Amidst these developments, suppliers with established ties to Chinese companies involved in the lithium sector seized the opportunity presented by the bans. Leveraging their strong relationships, they swiftly moved to establish processing factories within the affected countries. This strategic manoeuvre not only capitalized on existing partnerships but also aligned with the broader trend of moving up the value chain in the global lithium market.

As the years passed, the results of this strategic shift began to materialize. Domestic processing capacity increased, generating employment opportunities and fostering technological development within the countries. Furthermore, by adding value to their mineral exports through processing, these nations saw a significant boost in revenue and economic diversification. Additionally, the establishment of processing facilities attracted further investment and expertise, positioning these countries as emerging players in the global supply chain of critical minerals. In hindsight, what initially seemed like a controversial policy decision ultimately proved to be a catalyst for economic growth and industrial development in these resource-rich African nations. Strong supplier relationships play a crucial role in enhancing supply chain efficiency and driving innovation. By fostering collaboration, trust, and mutual support, businesses can optimize their procurement processes, reduce costs, and unlock new opportunities for product development and improvement.

Strong supplier relationships contribute to supply chain efficiency by enhancing communication and coordination. When businesses maintain close relationships with their suppliers, they can share information about inventory levels, demand forecasts, and production schedules more effectively. This enables suppliers to better anticipate their customers' needs and adjust their operations accordingly, reducing the risk of stock-outs, delays, and disruptions in the supply chain. Additionally, by collaborating closely with suppliers, businesses can identify and address potential bottlenecks or inefficiencies in the procurement process, streamlining operations and reducing lead times. Furthermore, strong supplier relationships can lead to cost savings and increased profitability. By developing long-term partnerships based on trust and mutual benefit, businesses can negotiate favourable terms, pricing, and payment terms with their suppliers. This can result in lower procurement costs, economies of scale, and improved cash flow management. Additionally, by working collaboratively to identify opportunities for cost reduction and process improvement, businesses and their suppliers can drive continuous efficiency gains throughout the supply chain, further enhancing profitability and competitiveness.

Moreover, strong supplier relationships foster a culture of innovation and continuous improvement. When businesses view their suppliers as strategic partners rather than mere transactional vendors, they can leverage their suppliers' expertise, capabilities, and resources to drive innovation and differentiation in their products and services. By collaborating on product design, materials selection, and process optimization, businesses and their suppliers can co- create innovative solutions that meet customer needs more effectively and differentiate the brand in the marketplace. Additionally, by fostering a culture of innovation and knowledge sharing within the supply chain, businesses can tap into the collective wisdom and creativity of their suppliers, driving continuous improvement and staying ahead of the competition. In addition to driving operational efficiency and innovation, strong supplier relationships also contribute to risk mitigation and resilience in the supply chain. By building trust and transparency with their suppliers, businesses can proactively identify and address potential risks, such as supply shortages, quality issues, or geopolitical disruptions. Additionally, by diversifying their supplier base and developing alternative sourcing options, businesses can reduce their dependence on any single supplier and mitigate the impact of unforeseen disruptions or disasters.

Strong supplier relationships are essential for enhancing supply chain efficiency, driving innovation, and ensuring business success. By fostering collaboration, trust, and mutual support with their suppliers, businesses can improve communication and coordination, reduce costs, drive continuous improvement, and mitigate risks in the supply chain. In today's fast-paced and competitive business environment, investing in strong supplier relationships is not only a strategic imperative but also a key driver of sustainable growth and competitive advantage.

9.

Financial Networks: Relationship Capital

Once revered for its stability and profitability, Saudi Aramco faced a tumultuous period in 2020 as global oil prices plummeted amidst a perfect storm of pandemic-induced disruptions and geopolitical tensions. Doubts arose among investors, including prominent names like BlackRock and Vanguard, about the company's ability to weather the crisis. However, through rigorous cost-cutting measures and strategic diversification efforts, Saudi Aramco demonstrated resilience, ultimately stabilizing as oil prices recovered and the global economy showed signs of revival. As confidence in Saudi Aramco's prospects was reignited, investors reaffirmed their commitment to the company's long-term value. The sentiment echoed across the investment community underscored Saudi Aramco's status as a cornerstone of many portfolios. With plans to boost dividends and pursue strategic growth opportunities, Saudi Aramco reaffirmed its position as a beacon of stability in the volatile energy sector landscape, currently maintaining its status as one of the world's largest and most valuable companies. Building strong relationships with investors and financiers is paramount for business stability and growth, particularly in African business contexts where access to capital and investment opportunities can be limited. These relationships not only provide essential funding but also offer strategic guidance, credibility, and networking opportunities that can fuel business expansion and success.

One significant impact of building strong relationships with investors and financiers is increased access to capital. In many African countries, access to traditional bank financing can be challenging due to stringent lending criteria, limited banking infrastructure, and high interest rates. As a result, businesses often rely on alternative sources of funding, such as venture capital, private equity, impact investing, and angel investors. By cultivating strong relationships with these investors, businesses can access the capital they need to fund their operations, expand their market reach, and invest in innovation and growth initiatives. For example, in Nigeria, start-ups in the tech sector such as Paystack and Flutterwave have attracted significant investment from international venture capital firms like Y Combinator and Sequoia Capital, enabling them to scale rapidly and become market leaders in the Fintech space. Building strong relationships with investors and financiers can enhance business stability by providing a cushion against economic downturns or unforeseen challenges. In African economies characterized by volatility, political instability, and currency fluctuations, businesses often face heightened risks and uncertainties that can threaten their survival.

Having supportive investors who provide not only financial backing but also strategic guidance and mentorship can help businesses navigate these challenges more effectively. For instance, during the COVID-19 pandemic, many African businesses faced disruptions to their operations and cash flow. Those with strong investor relationships were better positioned to weather the storm by accessing additional funding, renegotiating terms with creditors, and adapting their business models to changing market conditions.

Investors often bring more than just capital to the table; they also offer industry expertise, market insights, and valuable networks that can open doors to new customers, partners, and distribution channels. For example, in South Africa, Naspers, a multinational internet and media group, has played a pivotal role in supporting the growth of numerous technology start-ups across the continent through its investment arm, Naspers Foundry. By providing not only funding but also access to its extensive network and resources, Naspers has enabled these start-ups scale their operations, expand into new markets, and achieve sustainable growth. In addition to financial support, strong relationships with investors and financiers can enhance a business's credibility and reputation in the market. Investors often conduct thorough due diligence before committing capital to a business, assessing factors such as the management team, market opportunity, competitive positioning, and growth prospects. By securing investment from reputable investors or financial institutions, businesses can validate their business model, build trust with customers and partners, and attract additional investment and support from other stakeholders. For example, in Kenya, companies like M-KOPA Solar and Twiga Foods have gained international recognition and investor backing for their innovative business models and positive social impact, leading to further investment and expansion opportunities. Building strong relationships with investors and financiers is essential for business stability and growth in African contexts. These relationships provide access to capital, strategic guidance, networking opportunities, and credibility that can fuel business expansion and success. By cultivating supportive investor relationships, businesses can navigate economic challenges, unlock growth opportunities, and achieve their full potential in dynamic and competitive markets across the continent.

10.

Internal Networks: Enhancing Organizational Cohesion

Fostering strong internal relationships is crucial for building a cohesive and motivated workforce that drives organizational success.

In George Orwell's allegorical novel "Animal Farm," Napoleon the pig serves as a symbol of the manipulation of power and the importance of fostering internal relationships. As the story unfolds, Napoleon gradually consolidates control over the other animals on the farm, using fear and manipulation to maintain his authority. One illustrative scene occurs when Napoleon begins to rewrite history, altering the farm's commandments to justify his actions and further consolidate his power. Despite the initial confusion and dissent among the animals, Napoleon's manipulation of information and control over communication channels ultimately undermine their unity and cohesion. This example underscores the importance of fostering open communication and maintaining transparency within organizations. When leaders prioritize internal relationships built on trust and collaboration, they create an environment where employees feel empowered to speak up and hold leadership accountable, preventing the erosion of trust and the abuse of power. A harmonious workplace culture characterized by trust, collaboration, and mutual respect lays the foundation for employee engagement, productivity, and retention. By prioritizing internal relationships, organizations can create an environment where employees feel valued, supported, and empowered to contribute their best work. One of the key benefits of fostering strong internal relationships is improved communication and collaboration among team members. When employees feel comfortable sharing ideas, asking for help, and providing feedback to one another, teamwork flourishes, and collective goals are achieved more effectively. A culture of open communication fosters creativity, innovation, and problem-solving, as diverse perspectives are welcomed and respected. For example, in a software development team, strong internal relationships enable programmers, designers, and quality assurance engineers to collaborate seamlessly, resulting in high-quality products delivered on time and within budget.

Strong internal relationships also contribute to a positive work environment where employees feel supported and valued by their peers and supervisors. When colleagues form meaningful connections and show genuine care and concern for each other's well- being, morale and job satisfaction increase. Employees are more likely to feel motivated to come to work, engage in their tasks, and go the extra mile to help their team succeed. For instance, in a customer service team, strong internal relationships create a sense of camaraderie and shared purpose, leading to higher levels of job satisfaction and lower rates of turnover. Furthermore, fostering strong internal relationships promotes a culture of trust and accountability within the organization. When employees trust their colleagues and managers to act with integrity, honesty, and fairness, they are more likely to take ownership of their work, make informed decisions, and uphold high standards of performance. Trust also encourages transparency and openness, as employees feel comfortable sharing information and admitting mistakes without fear of judgment or reprisal. For example, in a sales team, strong internal relationships based on trust enable sales representatives to collaborate effectively, share leads and best practices, and work together towards common sales targets.

As trust and cohesion are undermined in Napoleon's kingdom, the once-united animal community begins to fragment, with suspicion and resentment festering among the ranks. Discontent grows as Napoleon consolidates power, leading to internal strife and division. Without a foundation of trust and mutual respect, the animals become disillusioned and disengaged, their productivity and morale plummeting.

Ultimately, the kingdom descends into chaos and tyranny, with Napoleon ruling through fear and oppression, highlighting the catastrophic consequences of neglecting internal relationships and fostering a culture of distrust and division. In addition to improving communication, collaboration, and trust, fostering strong internal relationships can also lead to increased employee engagement and retention. When employees feel connected to their colleagues and the organization as a whole, they are more likely to be emotionally invested in their work and committed to its success. Engaged employees are more productive, creative, and resilient in the face of challenges, contributing to higher levels of organizational performance and competitiveness. Moreover, strong internal relationships reduce the likelihood of turnover by creating a sense of loyalty and belonging among employees. For example, in a marketing team, strong internal relationships foster a supportive and inclusive culture where employees feel valued for their contributions, leading to higher levels of job satisfaction and retention. Fostering strong internal relationships is essential for building a cohesive and motivated workforce that drives organizational success. By prioritizing communication, collaboration, trust, and engagement among employees, organizations can create a positive work environment where individuals thrive and contribute their best work. Investing in internal relationships not only improves team dynamics and performance but also enhances employee satisfaction, retention, and overall organizational effectiveness.

II.

External Networks: Expanding Influence and Reach

Dr. James Mulwana, a revered Ugandan entrepreneur and business champion in East Africa, left an indelible mark on Uganda's manufacturing landscape through his visionary leadership at Nice House of Plastics. Established in the early 1970s, Nice House of Plastics began as a modest producer of plastic household items under Dr. Mulwana's leadership. Through his emphasis on strategic networking and innovation, the company rapidly ascended to become a leading player in Uganda's plastics industry. Recognizing the importance of strong relationships and partnerships, Dr. Mulwana forged alliances with local and international manufacturers, ensuring a steady supply of raw materials and cutting-edge production technologies. Leveraging his extensive network within Uganda's business and political spheres, he navigated regulatory challenges and expanded the company's market reach into regional markets, solidifying its influence in East Africa.

Dr. Mulwana's legacy as an entrepreneurial visionary lives on through Nice House of Plastics, a testament to the transformative power of strategic networking and innovative leadership in driving business growth and sustainability in Uganda and beyond. Expanding market reach and influence within an industry often relies on effective network utilization, leveraging connections to amplify brand presence, access new markets, and foster collaborations. Business depth hinges not only on the quality of products or services but also on the ability to reach and influence a wider audience. Utilizing networks strategically has become a cornerstone of modern business practices, offering unparalleled opportunities for expansion and growth. Building strong networks begins with identifying key stakeholders, from industry peers and suppliers to customers and influencers. Cultivating meaningful relationships within these circles fosters trust and opens doors to new opportunities. Networking events, industry conferences, and online platforms such as LinkedIn are valuable tools for forging connections. Collaborating with complementary businesses or industry leaders can significantly broaden market reach. By pooling resources and expertise, companies can access new customer segments, enter untapped markets, and drive innovation. Strategic partnerships also lend credibility and authority to brands, enhancing their influence within the industry.

Digital platforms offer unprecedented reach and scalability for businesses looking to expand their market presence. Social media platforms, content marketing, and influencer collaborations are powerful tools for engaging with audiences and building brand awareness. Leveraging data analytics allows companies to target specific demographics effectively, maximizing the impact of their digital marketing efforts.

Active participation in industry-specific communities and forums fosters relationships with like-minded individuals and organizations. By providing valuable insights, sharing expertise, and offering support, companies can position themselves as thought leaders and trusted authorities within their respective fields.

Engaging with communities also facilitates word-of-mouth referrals and grassroots advocacy, amplifying brand influence organically. The landscape of business and networking is constantly evolving, necessitating a commitment to continuous learning and adaptation. Staying abreast of industry trends, emerging technologies, and shifting consumer behaviours enables companies to remain relevant and competitive. Flexibility and agility are key to navigating the dynamic nature of network utilization effectively. Through continuous innovation and a commitment to quality, Nice House of Plastics expanded its product range to meet the diverse needs of its customers, from household items to industrial packaging solutions. By strategically utilizing its networks, the company not only secured its position as a market leader in Uganda but also ventured into regional markets, further solidifying its influence in the East African region. Utilizing networks to expand market reach and influence in the industry is not merely a strategy but a fundamental aspect of modern business operations. By building strong relationships, fostering collaborations, harnessing digital platforms, engaging with communities, and embracing continuous learning, companies can position themselves for sustained growth and success in an increasingly interconnected world.

12.

Technology and Networks: Enhancing Human Connections

In recent years, a transformative wave has swept across various nations, reshaping the traditional landscape of the workweek. It all began with pioneering companies in Sweden, such as the technology start-up Brath and the retirement home Svartedalen, who dared to challenge the conventional 9-to-5 grind by implementing six-hour workdays. Inspired by their success, other Scandinavian countries like Norway followed suit, with companies in the construction sector, like the Skanska Norway Group, experimenting with shorter workweeks, shifting from the standard five days to four. As the movement gained momentum, Finland emerged as a trailblazer in the quest for a better work- life balance. Companies like the software firm Reaktor and the insurance company SITRA piloted a four-day workweek, allowing employees to enjoy longer weekends and recharge. Meanwhile, on the opposite side of the globe, in New Zealand, businesses like Perpetual Guardian led the charge, embracing a four- day workweek with full pay, reporting increased productivity and improved employee satisfaction. Amidst these global shifts, Japan embarked on its own journey towards work reform, grappling with issues of overwork and burnout. Companies like Microsoft Japan implemented a four-day workweek, witnessing a 40% boost in productivity. Throughout this transformative period, technology emerged as a crucial enabler, ensuring seamless workflow and connectivity despite reduced hours. Advanced communication tools and remote collaboration platforms became the backbone of this new era, empowering employees to thrive in a more flexible and balanced work environment.

Technology offers a plethora of tools and platforms that can be leveraged to strengthen and maintain business relationships in various ways. Let's explore: Customer Relationship Management (CRM) Systems centralize customer data, interactions, and transactions, allowing businesses to better understand and cater to their customers' needs. By tracking communication history, preferences, and purchase behavior, companies can personalize interactions and provide tailored solutions, thereby fostering stronger relationships.

Email marketing platforms enable businesses to send targeted, personalized messages to customers and prospects at scale. Automation features allow for the scheduling of follow-up emails, birthday greetings, and promotional campaigns, ensuring consistent communication and nurturing of relationships over time.

Social media platforms serve as valuable channels for engaging with customers and prospects on a more personal level. Businesses can use social media to share valuable content, respond to inquiries in real- time, and showcase their brand personality, thereby building rapport and trust with their audience. With the rise of remote work and virtual communication tools, businesses can easily connect with clients and partners regardless of geographical barriers. Virtual meetings and webinars enable face- to-face interactions, fostering deeper relationships through meaningful discussions and collaborations.

Collaboration platforms such as Slack,

Microsoft Teams, and Google Workspace facilitate seamless communication and collaboration among team members, clients, and partners. By streamlining workflows and enabling real-time collaboration on projects, these tools strengthen relationships through enhanced productivity and efficiency. Leveraging data analytics and artificial intelligence, businesses can deliver personalized content and product recommendations based on customers' past behavior and preferences. By providing relevant and timely information, companies demonstrate their understanding of customers' needs and interests, thereby deepening their relationship with them. Technology enables businesses to gather feedback and insights from customers through online surveys, feedback forms, and review platforms. By actively soliciting feedback and demonstrating responsiveness to customer concerns, businesses can show that they value their opinions and are committed to continuous improvement, thus strengthening their relationships with customers. European companies like Zalando, Lufthansa, and IKEA have implemented strategies to actively solicit feedback and demonstrate responsiveness to customer concerns. Zalando, founded in 2008, collects feedback through surveys and social media, fostering a reputation for excellent customer service and increasing loyalty. Lufthansa, with a long-standing commitment to feedback, encourages passengers to share their experiences, leading to service improvements and higher satisfaction levels. IKEA, since its inception in the 1940s, prioritizes customer feedback through various channels, resulting in enhanced brand reputation, better product offerings, and stronger customer relationships. These strategies yield benefits such as increased customer satisfaction and loyalty, improved brand perception, better product development, and higher profitability. Overall, by leveraging technology effectively, businesses can streamline communication, personalize interactions, gather insights, and foster collaboration, all of which contribute to building and maintaining strong and lasting relationships with customers, partners, and stakeholders.

13.

Global Networking: Crossing Borders and Cultures

In the vast tapestry of global business, where cultures interweave and opportunities abound, the journey of the Global Opportunities Committee of the Atlanta Black Chambers is a tale of vision and connection. Under the stewardship of Ricardo Berris, the Committee embarked on a quest to embrace the rich diversity of cultures spanning the Caribbean, Asia, Oceania, Western, Arabic and native African regions. With a keen understanding that meaningful interactions are the bedrock of business prowess in our globalized economy, the Committee set out to bridge divides and foster alliances. They meticulously appointed regional representatives across the globe, each tasked with advancing the corporate agenda and nurturing Black businesses worldwide. Fuelled by innovation, they orchestrated online business-to- business matchmaking events, where participants from diverse backgrounds found common ground and forged functional partnerships across continents. Yet, their journey didn't end there; instead, it blossomed into a series of transformative initiatives. From investor delegations crisscrossing African nations like South Africa, Botswana, Zimbabwe, and Zambia, to business visits to Colombia and the Caribbean, the Committee nurtured multi-faceted partnerships that transcended borders. Through their unwavering support and guidance, participants and members were empowered to deepen their regional reach and promote their corporate agenda with vigor. What is envisaged out of this tapestry of collaboration is a phenomenon—a wave of Black-owned businesses taking shape across the globe, united by a singular purpose. With networks established and bridges built, a renaissance of businesses within the global Black community awaits, poised to redefine the landscape of entrepreneurship with diversity, resilience, and unity at its core.

Cultural Sensitivity and Adaptation
One of the primary challenges in international

relationship-building is navigating cultural differences. Cultural norms regarding communication styles, hierarchy, decision-making, and business etiquette vary significantly across countries. Therefore, it is essential for businesses to demonstrate cultural sensitivity and adaptability. This involves investing time and resources in cross-cultural training for employees, learning about the customs and traditions of the target market, and respecting local norms and protocols. By understanding and appreciating cultural differences, businesses can avoid misunderstandings and forge deeper connections with international partners and clients.

Effective Communication

Effective communication is the cornerstone of successful international relationships. Language barriers, time zone differences, and technological limitations can hinder communication efforts in a global context. Utilizing multilingual staff, interpreters, and translation services can help bridge the language gap. Additionally, leveraging technology such as video conferencing, instant messaging, and collaboration tools facilitates real-time communication across borders. Clear and concise communication, coupled with active listening, ensures that messages are understood accurately and fosters trust and transparency in international business relationships.

Building Trust and Credibility

Trust is essential in any business relationship, but it takes on added significance in an international context where partners may be geographically distant and unfamiliar with each other's business practices. Building trust requires consistent and reliable behavior, delivering on promises, and demonstrating integrity and transparency in all dealings. Investing time in face-to-face meetings, establishing personal connections, and honouring commitments are key strategies for building trust in international business relationships. Moreover, maintaining open lines of communication and addressing concerns promptly helps to reinforce trust and credibility over time.

Cultivating Personal Relationships

John Hope Bryant said, "Your relationships will in many ways determine your economic condition". In many cultures, business is conducted based on personal relationships rather than purely transactional interactions. Therefore, investing in building personal connections with international partners and clients can yield significant dividends. This may involve socializing outside of work, attending cultural events, or exchanging gifts as a sign of respect and goodwill. By nurturing personal relationships, businesses can establish a strong foundation of trust and loyalty that transcends business transactions and fosters long-term partnerships.

Adapting to Local Market Dynamics

Fanta tastes different in Europe and America because of where it's made and what people like to drink there. In Europe, they often use sugar to make it sweet, while in America, they might use something called high fructose corn syrup. Companies like Coca-Cola, who make Fanta, have to change the recipe a bit to match what people in each place like. They also have to follow the rules about what ingredients they can use. So, when you try Fanta in different countries, it might taste a little different because of these things. It's like how your mom might make spaghetti one way, and your friend's mom might make it another way—they both taste good, but they're a little different. Successful international relationship-building requires a deep understanding of the local market dynamics, including regulatory environments, consumer preferences, and competitive landscapes. Businesses must be willing to adapt their products, services, and marketing strategies to align with local needs and preferences. This may involve customizing offerings, pricing strategies, and distribution channels to suit the specific requirements of each market. By demonstrating a commitment to understanding and addressing the unique challenges and opportunities of the local market, businesses can earn the trust and loyalty of international partners and clients.

Building and maintaining relationships in an international business context is a complex yet rewarding endeavour. By embracing cultural sensitivity, effective communication, trust-building, personal connections, and market adaptation, businesses can overcome the challenges of global expansion and forge mutually beneficial partnerships that drive long-term success in the global marketplace. Building strong international relationships is not only essential for business growth but also for fostering understanding and collaboration across borders in an increasingly interconnected world.

14.

Resilience through Relationships: Navigating Crises

Amidst the COVID-19 lockdown in Africa, a narrative of resilience unfolded as businesses united to weather the storm. In Lagos, TechSavvy Health collaborated with CareWell Hospitals to launch TeleCare Africa, providing remote medical consultations. Across Kenya, AgriProduce Ltd. and Express Logistics ensured food security by swiftly transporting fresh produce from farms to markets. In Johannesburg, ProTech Industries partnered with SuperMart Retail to manufacture and distribute essential items like masks and sanitizers. As economies strained, EduFund Bank and LearnWell Foundation joined forces to support students through the EduCare Initiative. Meanwhile, in Tanzania, Safari Adventures, Cultural Gems Association, and the

Ministry of Tourism promoted domestic tourism, reviving local economies. Through these collaborations, businesses not only navigated the challenges of the pandemic but also emerged stronger, showcasing the power of unity amidst adversity. The role of robust networks in helping businesses navigate and recover from crises cannot be overstated. In times of uncertainty and disruption, such as natural disasters, economic downturns, or global pandemics, businesses with strong networks are better equipped to weather the storm and emerge stronger on the other side. Robust networks provide businesses with access to a wide range of resources and support mechanisms that are invaluable during times of crisis. Whether it's financial assistance, expertise, manpower, or essential supplies, businesses with strong networks can tap into a diverse pool of contacts and partners to address immediate needs and mitigate the impact of the crisis. Collaborative networks, industry associations, and government agencies often play a crucial role in facilitating resource sharing and coordination efforts, enabling businesses to navigate through challenging times more effectively. Timely and accurate information is essential for making informed decisions during a crisis. Robust networks serve as conduits for information sharing and knowledge exchange among businesses, industry peers, and relevant stakeholders. Through communication channels such as industry forums, online communities, and professional networks, businesses can stay updated on emerging trends, regulatory changes, market dynamics, and best practices for crisis management. This access to real- time information enables businesses to adapt their strategies quickly, identify emerging opportunities, and mitigate potential risks.

In times of crisis, collaboration becomes essential for businesses to pool their resources, expertise, and capabilities to overcome shared challenges. Robust networks facilitate collaboration and mutual assistance among businesses, enabling them to leverage each other's strengths and support one another through difficult times. Strategic partnerships, joint ventures, and informal alliances allow businesses to share risks, innovate solutions, and explore new market opportunities collectively. By working together, businesses can enhance their resilience, accelerate recovery efforts, and emerge from the crisis stronger and more resilient than before. Diversifying market presence and supply chain networks is key to reducing vulnerability to external shocks and disruptions. Businesses with robust networks are better positioned to diversify their customer base, distribution channels, and sourcing options, thereby spreading risk and minimizing the impact of a crisis on their operations. Through international partnerships, trade agreements, and global alliances, businesses can access new markets, reduce dependence on single suppliers or markets, and build resilience against geopolitical, economic, or environmental uncertainties.

Maintaining trust and credibility with stakeholders is crucial for businesses navigating through a crisis. Robust networks enable businesses to engage with customers, employees, investors, regulators, and the broader community in transparent and proactive communication. By keeping stakeholders informed, addressing concerns promptly, and demonstrating resilience and adaptability, businesses can safeguard their reputation and mitigate reputational damage during a crisis. Moreover, strong relationships with stakeholders built over time through consistent engagement and mutual trust serve as a valuable asset in facilitating recovery efforts and rebuilding confidence in the business's ability to overcome adversity. Evidently, robust networks play a pivotal role in helping businesses navigate and recover from crises by providing access to resources, facilitating information sharing and collaboration, enabling market diversification and risk mitigation, and supporting reputation management and stakeholder engagement. By leveraging their networks effectively, businesses can enhance their resilience, adaptability, and agility in the face of adversity, ultimately emerging stronger and more resilient from crises. Investing in building and nurturing robust networks is therefore essential for businesses looking to thrive in an increasingly uncertain and interconnected world.

15.

The Future of Business: The Evolving Role of Networks

The rapidly evolving business landscape today underscores the necessity of having the ability to cultivate and maintain strong networks and relationships for long-term success of a business. As technology continues to reshape the way we connect and interact, businesses must anticipate future trends in networking and relationship management to stay ahead of the curve and remain competitive.

Businesses globally are adapting to the changing landscape by implementing various strategies in networking and relationship management. In China, for instance, companies are leveraging digital platforms like WeChat and Alibaba's ecosystem not only for marketing but also for building and nurturing relationships with customers and partners. Tencent, the company behind WeChat, utilizes its vast user base to facilitate interactions between businesses and consumers, offering features like customer service chatbots and personalized recommendations. In India, firms are embracing social media and online communities to foster connections and engage with stakeholders. The Tata Group, utilizes its social media presence not just for brand promotion but also for engaging with customers, gathering feedback, and addressing concerns promptly. Others like OYO Rooms have prioritized relationship management by offering personalized experiences and loyalty programs to their customers. Businesses are tapping into emerging technologies like blockchain to enhance transparency and trust in relationships. Vezeeta, a healthcare startup based in Egypt, uses blockchain technology to secure medical records and streamline communication between patients, doctors, and insurance providers. This not only improves efficiency but also strengthens trust among stakeholders in the healthcare ecosystem. This is the undeniable future; companies across the globe are leveraging technology and innovative strategies to cultivate and maintain strong networks and relationships to stay afloat in today and tomorrow's business landscape.

Rise of Virtual Networking Platforms

With the proliferation of remote work and digital communication tools, virtual networking platforms are gaining traction as viable alternatives to traditional in-person networking events. These platforms leverage technology such as artificial intelligence (AI) and virtual reality (VR) to facilitate meaningful connections and interactions in a virtual environment. By offering features such as matchmaking algorithms, interactive discussions, and virtual meetups, these platforms enable businesses to expand their networks and forge valuable relationships without the limitations of geographical barriers.

Emphasis on Personalization and Customization

As consumers become increasingly inundated with generic marketing messages, the demand for personalized and customized experiences is on the rise. In the realm of networking and relationship management, businesses must tailor their interactions and communications to meet the specific needs and preferences of their audience. This may involve leveraging data analytics and AI-driven insights to deliver targeted content, recommendations, and experiences that resonate with individual stakeholders. By prioritizing personalization, businesses can deepen their connections with customers, partners, and stakeholders, ultimately driving greater loyalty and engagement.

Integration of Blockchain Technology

Blockchain technology has the potential to revolutionize networking and relationship management by providing a secure and transparent platform for managing transactions and data exchange. In the context of business relationships, blockchain-based systems can facilitate trust and transparency by recording and verifying interactions in a tamper-proof manner. Smart contracts, which are self-executing contracts with the terms of the agreement directly written into code, can automate and streamline processes such as contract management, payments, and dispute resolution, reducing friction and enhancing efficiency in business relationships.

Shift towards Community-Centric Engagement

Businesses are increasingly recognizing the value of building and nurturing communities around their brands, products, and services. Rather than focusing solely on transactional relationships, companies are investing in fostering authentic connections and fostering a sense of belonging among their stakeholders. This community-centric approach to relationship management involves creating spaces for collaboration, knowledge-sharing, and peer support, whether through online forums, social media groups, or exclusive membership programs. By cultivating communities around their brand, businesses can foster deeper loyalty, advocacy, and engagement among their audience, driving long-term success and sustainability.

Nike has built a global community of athletes, fitness enthusiasts, and sneakerheads through various initiatives such as NikePlus membership program, Nike Run Club, and Nike Training Club app.

The NikePlus membership program offers exclusive access to product launches, personalized training plans, and member-only events, fostering a sense of belonging and exclusivity among its members. The Nike Run Club and Nike Training Club app provide users with free access to training resources, challenges, and community forums, encouraging users to connect with like-minded individuals, share their fitness journeys, and support each other's goals. By creating these platforms and initiatives, Nike not only strengthens its relationship with customers but also builds a loyal and engaged community around its brand. This community-driven approach not only drives posterity and sustainability but also helps Nike stay relevant in an ever-changing market landscape.

Augmented Reality (AR) and Mixed Reality (MR)

Augmented reality (AR) and mixed reality (MR) technologies are poised to transform networking and relationship management by providing immersive and interactive experiences that transcend physical boundaries. These technologies enable businesses to create virtual environments where users can engage with products, services, and content in a more immersive and engaging manner. In the context of relationship management, AR and MR can be used to host virtual events, product demonstrations, and training sessions, allowing businesses to connect with stakeholders in new and innovative ways. By embracing AR and MR, businesses can differentiate themselves from competitors and create memorable experiences that leave a lasting impression on their audience. Through their "Wheels" app, Canadian Tire allows customers to virtually try on tires using AR technology. Customers can see how different tire options will look on their vehicles, enabling them to make more informed purchasing decisions. Emirates Airlines is embracing AR technology to enhance the travel experience for its passengers. Emirates' "Emirates AR" app enables users to explore the interior of Emirates' Airbus A380 and Boeing 777 aircraft in 3D using AR technology. Passengers can virtually walk through cabins, explore seating options, and even book their preferred seats, providing them with a unique and immersive preview of their flight experience. Conversely, anticipating future trends in networking and relationship management is essential for businesses looking to stay ahead of the curve and maintain a competitive edge in today's dynamic business environment. By embracing emerging technologies, prioritizing personalization, fostering community-centric engagement, and leveraging blockchain technology, businesses can cultivate strong networks and relationships that drive long-term success and sustainability. As the business landscape continues to evolve, businesses must remain agile and adaptable, continuously innovating and evolving their approaches to networking and relationship management to meet the evolving needs and expectations of their stakeholders.

Conclusion

In the dynamic landscape of business, where competition is fierce and challenges abound, entrepreneurs and business leaders are constantly seeking the edge that will propel their ventures to success. While traditional metrics such as financial capital, human resources, physical assets, and knowledge have long been considered the cornerstone of business strategy, there is a resource that often goes overlooked but holds unparalleled potential: networks and relationships. Throughout this exploration, we have delved into the myriad ways in which networks and relationships serve as the linchpin of business success. From the ability to forge enduring connections with customers, suppliers, and investors to the intrinsic value of internal cohesion and external influence, networks and relationships permeate every facet of the entrepreneurial journey. In comparing networks and relationships to other business resources, it becomes clear that their significance transcends mere utility; they embody the lifeblood of enterprise. While financial resources may enable transactions, it is the trust and reciprocity forged through relationships that underpin lasting partnerships and drive sustainable growth. Human resources provide the skills and expertise necessary for innovation and execution, yet it is the collaborative networks and supportive relationships that amplify their impact and harness their full potential. Physical assets may confer tangible advantages, but it is the connections and networks that imbue them with strategic value, facilitating access to markets, resources, and opportunities. Knowledge, once considered the ultimate currency of business, finds its true worth in the networks through which it flows, enriching the collective wisdom of individuals and organizations alike.

As we reflect on the lessons gleaned from this discourse, it becomes abundantly clear why every entrepreneur and business leader must accord paramount importance to networks and relationships. In an interconnected world where success is contingent upon collaboration, adaptability, and resilience, the ability to cultivate and leverage robust networks is not merely advantageous, it is imperative. By investing in the cultivation of meaningful relationships, entrepreneurs and business leaders can unlock a wealth of opportunities, fortify their enterprises against adversity, and forge a path toward sustainable growth and prosperity. To neglect the cultivation of networks and relationships is to forsake one of the most potent sources of competitive advantage in the modern business landscape. As we stand on the precipice of a new era defined by connectivity and collaboration, let us heed the lessons of "The Thumb Resource" and recognize that true success lies not in the accumulation of resources, but in the strength of the connections we forge and the relationships we nurture. In embracing networks and relationships as the cornerstone of their endeavours, entrepreneurs and business leaders will discover a reservoir of untapped potential—a resource more valuable than gold, more enduring than steel, and more indispensable than any other. It is in the cultivation of these connections that the seeds of innovation are sown, the bonds of trust are forged, and the fabric of success is woven. May we, as stewards of enterprise, recognize the profound significance of networks and relationships, and may we cultivate them with the care and reverence they so rightfully deserve.

www.ingramcontent.com/pod-product-compliance
Lightning Source LLC
Chambersburg PA
CBHW050317230526
45471CB00005B/2227